THE TRIGGE LIBRARY

ST. WULFRAM'S CHURCH
GRANTHAM

A GUIDE

by
Brian Stagg, *Custos*

Independent Publishing Network

First published in 2021 by Independent Publishing Network

Text © Brian Stagg 2021
Photos © Roger Sleigh 2021 unless otherwise stated

The right of Brian Stagg to be identified as the
Author of this publication has been asserted by him
in accordance with the Copyright, Designs and Patents Act 1988.

All rights reserved

No part of this publication may be reproduced, stored in any retrieval system or transmitted in any form, electronic or mechanical, including photocopying, or by any means without written permission from the author.

ISBN: 978-1-80049-293-6

A CIP catalogue record for this work is available from the British Library

Designed in the UK by The Artworker, Nottingham
Printed in the UK by Flexpress Ltd, Leicester

Supported by the Friends of St Wulfram's Church (Charity No. 1066896)

CONTENTS

PREFACE	5
PROLOGUE	7
THE LIBRARY	9
THE FOUNDER	15
THE BOOKS	21
EPILOGUE	33
ACKNOWLEDGEMENTS	35

PREFACE

I feel very fortunate to be the Rector of St Wulfram's Church in Grantham, which attracts many hundreds of visitors every year from both the UK and across the world. What they will see was described by Simon Jenkins in his book *England's Thousand Best Churches* as 'one of the most exhilarating images of English Gothic' in the country. There are many interesting artefacts on show, both inside and outside the church, but perhaps the most valuable is the Library founded by Revd. Francis Trigge in 1598.

This was the first public reference library in Britain, open to anyone who could make use of its books, and I am sure that my Tudor predecessors would have benefitted from having such a resource available to assist with their studies. Both they and following generations were inspired and challenged by the works they found on its shelves.

Today it is a privilege and a blessing for us to care for this national treasure, and we are very grateful to Francis Trigge for his generous gift to the people of Grantham that added so much to the town's historic heritage. But it is also a great responsibility. Fortunately, we have a team of willing and knowledgeable volunteers who ensure that the Library is maintained and open for those who wish to see it.

This guide replaces an earlier publication by the late John Glenn who, together with David Walsh, produced the definitive catalogue of the collection in 1988. It now contains the results of much new research on the Library, its books, and the life and times of its founder.

Fr. Stuart Cradduck
Rector and Rural Dean of Grantham, St. Wulfram's and Vicar of St. John the Evangelist, Manthorpe.
January 2021

PROLOGUE

In 1467 Johann von Speyer made an important decision that would have a profound effect on his future. He had worked for many years in Mainz, first as a goldsmith and latterly as a printer's apprentice; but now the time had come for him to set up his own business as a printer. However, the unstable financial situation that had plagued the city for decades made obtaining the necessary capital to start a new commercial venture very difficult. So, Johann looked to Venice, the greatest and most powerful city-state in Europe. Although the art of printing was spreading rapidly across the continent, he discovered that – in spite of its wealth and influence – not a single printer was working in that city. This was a great opportunity, so in 1468 he left Mainz and travelled south with his wife, his children and his brother Wendelin (also a printer).

Johann established his print shop, possibly in the Fondaco dei Tedeschi (the German mercantile centre) near the Rialto Bridge, and was formally welcomed by the Doge, Cristoforo Moro, and the ruling Council. They generously granted him a five-year monopoly for the printing of books. The first book to be printed in the city (1469) was Cicero's *Epistolae ad Familiares*. This was followed by a second edition of the same book; the *editio princeps* of Pliny the Elder's *Naturalis Historia*; and the second printed edition of Livy's *Ab Urbe condita libri* in 1470. Then, later in the same year, during the printing of Augustine's *De civitate Dei*, Johann died. As a result, the contract that had been negotiated between the Council of Venice and Johann became null and void.

Wendelin assumed control of the business, continuing to operate until 1477 and producing more than seventy major works – principally Roman classics and writings of the Church Fathers. But it was Wendelin's success that would also be his undoing. Many printers, both local and from further afield, flocked to Venice to set up new businesses and by the turn of the century the city had become a major centre for the production of hand-press books. Among them were the French printer, Nicholas Jensen, who is best known for having devised the superb Roman type used to print the first Bible in Italian; and Theobald Manucci (better known as Aldus Manutius) who founded the famous Aldine Press and developed type to print in languages other than Latin, notably Greek. But competition was fierce and a number of these businesses failed. Wendelin's print shop was probably one of them.

It was in 1472 Wendelin printed the *Repetitiones disputationes necnon tractatus diversorum doctorum* of Lanfranc de Oriano (Fig. 1), written in heavily abbreviated legal Latin. This collection of reports of court proceedings heard in the cities of northern Italy (principally Siena, Padua and

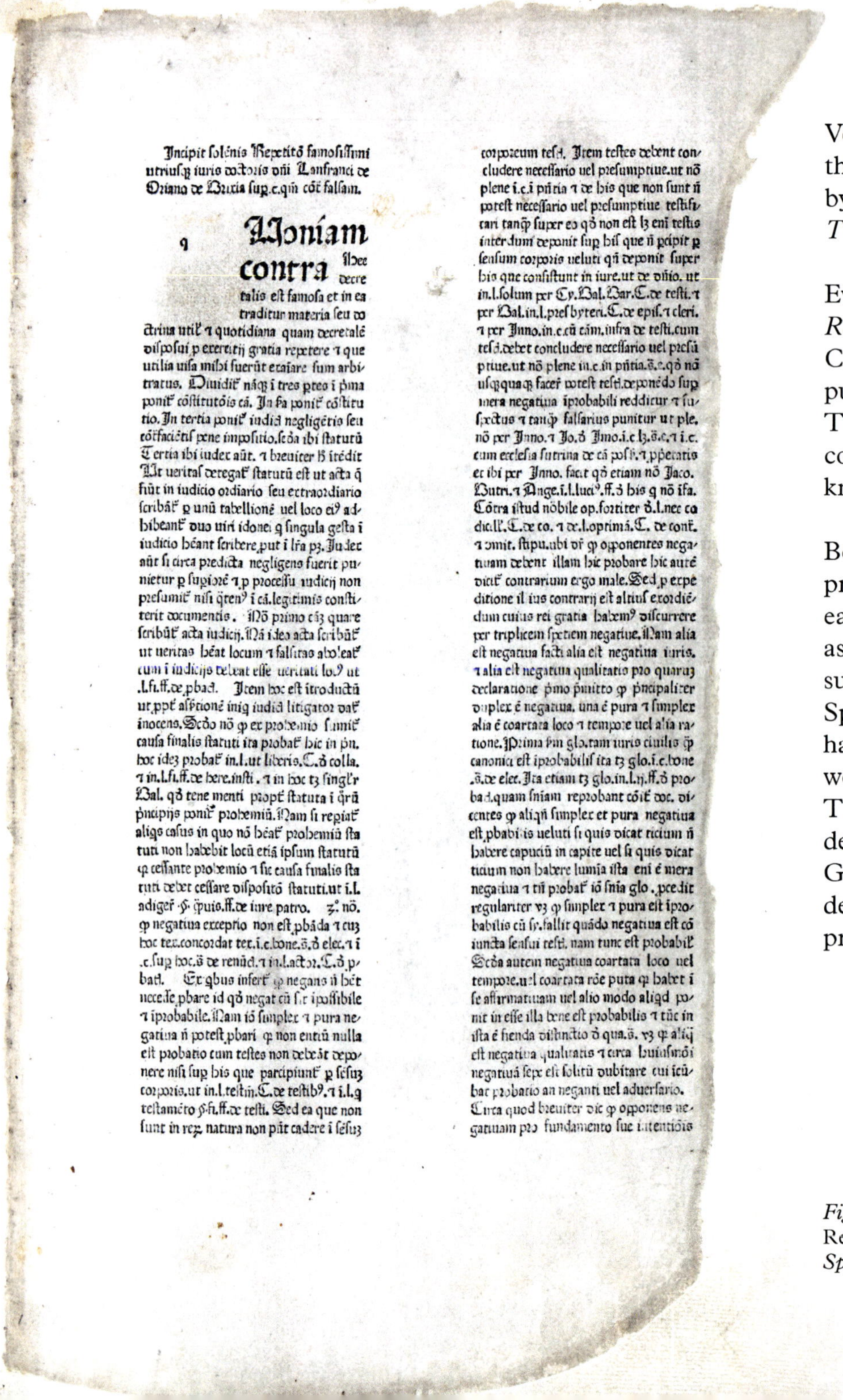
Incipit solēnis Repetitō famosissimi utriusq iuris doctoris dñi Lanfranci de Oriano de Brixia sup.c.qm cōt falsam.

Quoniam contra

Venice) predated by four years the first book printed in England by William Caxton – Chaucer's *The Canterbury Tales*.

Eventually a copy of the *Repetitiones* made its way to Cambridge, where it was purchased for the Trigge Library. This is the oldest book in the collection, and one of only 26 known to exist.

Both this book, and the Library, provide a direct link with the earliest days of printing, and serve as a reminder of those pioneers such as Johann and Wendelin von Speyer, whose determination and hard work ensured that books would be accessible more widely. They, and we, in turn, owe a debt of gratitude to Johannes Gutenberg of Mainz, whose development of the printing process made all this possible.

Fig. 1: A page from Lanfranc de Oriano's Repetitiones *printed by Wendelin von Speyer, Venice 1472.*

THE LIBRARY

The Trigge Library was founded in 1598 by Revd. Francis Trigge, the Rector of Welbourn, a village about thirteen miles north of Grantham. The papers relating to the foundation set out in detail Trigge's aim in establishing the Library, who had the responsibility for its security and maintenance and who should have access to it. On 20th October 1598 Trigge published an indenture from which three important points emerge:

- First, Trigge made clear that his purpose in founding the Library was 'for the encreasinge of learning and knowledge in divinitie and other liberall sciences', and that he 'hath provided or intendeth to provide at his like cost for the furnishing thereof, books of divinitie & other learning to the value of one hundereth poundes…'
- Second, although the library was housed in St. Wulfram's Church, Grantham, it was to be regarded as a civic foundation for which the Alderman and Burgesses of the town were responsible.
- Third, Trigge intended the library to be used by 'such of the clergie & others as well as beinge inhabitants in or near Grantham & the soake thereof as in other places in the said Countie'.

The Library is, therefore, the earliest public collection of books in England maintained by a civic authority and freely accessible to anybody who could benefit from it.

The indenture was signed and sealed by Trigge, the Alderman of Grantham, one of the two prebendaries of Salisbury Cathedral who held the Grantham livings, and their two vicars. It is lodged in the Lincolnshire Archives with another document, a schedule of rules, signed by the two vicars and the headmaster of the Grammar School (now the King's School).

The Library was sited in a room over the south porch of the church (Fig. 2), where it has remained for more than four hundred years. Before the Reformation, this provided accommodation for one of the two Grantham clergy, and has a fireplace, a facility for washing (*lavabo*) and a squint that gives a good view of the interior of the church (Fig 3). In the 1590s, when Trigge was seeking a secure place to house his Library, he found that the room was not in use. As visitors discover, it is only accessible via a narrow spiral staircase with stout wooden doors at the top and bottom. Trigge judged it to be ideal for his purpose, but required the permission of the Bishop of Lincoln for this change of use. The papers in the Lincolnshire Archives relating to the Library's

Fig. 2: The South Porch of St. Wulfram's Church, Grantham. The Trigge Library is located in a room over the entrance.

foundation are accompanied by an elaborate letter of consent in Latin for the use of the south porch room as a library, signed and dated in November 1599 by Bishop William Chadderton. The date of the Bishop's letter suggests that his tardiness in replying to Trigge's request probably delayed the opening of the Library until sometime in 1600.

In spite of the apparent security that the room provided, Trigge was still not entirely satisfied that the books would be safe, and so had them chained to the benches, reading desks and cabinets with which the room was furnished. In fact, Trigge's original schedule of rules required that the

Fig. 3: The north wall of the Library, showing the squint on the left, one of the book presses, and the lavabo *on the right.*

'bookes be kept continually bownd with convenient chaines to the staples devised and placed in the library for that purpose'. The chaining of books in libraries was not uncommon, the practice having its origins in medieval monasteries and convents where their removal for private use was often a problem. The chains in the Trigge Library were forged by a local blacksmith in wrought iron and are of exceptional quality (Fig. 4).

Typically, the chains were riveted to the edge of the front boards, so that the books were presented with the fore-edges of the pages outwards and the spines hidden, as can be seen today. Very few of the books in the Library have titles inscribed on their spines but, instead, have them hand-written on the page fore-edges. A number of volumes were added in the 17th century, including 13 books bequeathed to the Library in Trigge's will, but these were not chained.

Fig. 4: A close-up of some of the books, with the chains attached.

Trigge obtained the original books for his Library from Cambridge, known from several identifiable bindings associated with Cambridge binders. Three volumes were bound by Thomas Thomas and one by Garrett Godfrey, both well-known binders then working in that city. Further evidence lies in the signatures and marginalia added in early 16th century hands that can be traced to Cambridge. For example, the Library's copy of Duranti's *Rationale Divinorum Officiorum* was signed by William Irland of St. John's College, who died in 1571.

An agent was sent to Cambridge with a purse containing the 'one hundereth poundes or thereabouts' (more than £17,000 in modern money) as mentioned in the indenture, for which Trigge obtained about 230 volumes. The agent must have purchased most of the books in lots as his choice was, to say the least, indiscriminate. Of course, he brought back numerous books of religious interest: theological treatises, Bible commentaries, collections of sermons and Church histories. Together, they constitute a good, if eccentric, cross-section of the writings of those who supported or opposed the Reformation of the Church in the 16th century. However, there are also books on philosophy, zoology, cosmology, medicine, herbalism etc., as well as various versions of the Bible.

The instructional worth of some of the books to those who might have visited the Library in the 17th century is, at best, questionable. There are three large volumes of Catholic Canon Law with commentaries, dated 1488, 1505 and 1515, that would have been of little interest to readers from the towns and villages of rural Lincolnshire; and the same can be said of Lanfranc's *Repetitiones*, its excellent state of preservation probably due to the fact that it was rarely, if ever, opened.

No records exist to show who was using the Library in the decades following Francis Trigge's death. However, there may be a clue in the Grantham Hall Book relating to a donation made in 1642 by a local benefactor, Edward Skipwith. He gave fifty shillings for wood to be provided for a fire in the Library, allowing 'the viccars of Grantham in the winter and cold tyme of the yeare to follow their studdies'. No doubt, the 'viccars of Grantham' would have been grateful for his largess. It also seems likely that, in addition to the clergy, other visitors to the Library would have included pupils of the Grammar School, as the headmaster was one of three keyholders and would have had easy access to the collection. There is every likelihood that one of these pupils was Isaac Newton, who studied at the school between 1655 and 1661 before beginning his illustrious career at Trinity College, Cambridge.

Prior to Newton's time at the school the Library had been in some danger of complete destruction. Grantham was of strategic importance during the English Civil War (1642-1651), especially during the siege of Newark and its castle. Parliamentary soldiers did considerable damage to St. Wulfram's Church, using it as a stable for cavalry horses and burning and defacing the fabric. But, for some unknown reason, the Library avoided their attention.

The Library continued to attract donations of books during the 17th century. These included the works of the Neoplatonist philosopher Henry More, another former pupil of the Grammar School, which he donated sometime before 1685.

After the 17th century there is no further record of the Library until the 19th century, when it begins to be mentioned by local writers. A description of the Library in a directory of 1835 indicated that 'The books are generally in a very dilapidated state'.[1] In 1878 a series of letters

---

[1] Quoted in Roberts, A. (1971), *The chained library, Grantham.* Library History 2(3), 75-90.

appeared in the *Grantham Journal* that again expressed concern about the condition of the books and stressed the importance and value of the collection. In 1884, Samuel Bentley-Rudd, a churchwarden and builder, replaced the roof and floor of the room over the south porch, and constructed the three presses (bookcases) in which the books are now kept using wood from the original desks and other furniture in the Library. The rods to which the chains are now attached resemble those in the chained library of Hereford Cathedral.

When the work had been completed, Bentley-Rudd had a plaque placed on the east wall of the Library, with the inscription: 'To the Glory of God and in memory of Maud Bentley-Rudd who died in infancy in 1871 this porch and library were restored'. It serves as a lasting memorial both to his loss and his work.

Although the books were now protected from damp, nothing was done to restore them. Then, in 1893, Canon Hector Nelson retired from his post as Principal of the Lincoln Diocesan Training College (now Bishop Grosseteste University), and came to live in Grantham. He very quickly recognised that the books in the Library were in a dire condition and took responsibility for saving them from further decay. Together with William Mouncey, a local bookbinder, he repaired and restored almost two hundred volumes. It was through his prompt action that the survival of the Library was ensured.

Subsequently, a number of people have cared for the collection, sharing a common incentive about which John Glenn[2] wrote so eloquently: 'These ancient books, texts that once shaped the thinking of Europe, now link us always to that old benefactor [Francis Trigge] who so enriched our town when Elizabeth I still ruled. We owe it to our own past to keep them in good order and repair'.

---

2 Glenn, John (undated), *The Francis Trigge Library in St Wulfram's Church, Grantham.* Grantham: The Friends of St Wulfram's Church.

THE FOUNDER

The foundation of the Library was entirely in keeping with Francis Trigge's values and beliefs, and reflects his dedication to learning and the education of others. But what is known of this patron who contributed so generously to the cultural heritage of Grantham?

Trigge was born in 1547, the year Henry VIII died and was succeeded by his son who became Edward VI. Francis was the only child of Thomas Trigge and his wife Elizabeth (née Metcalf or Medcalfe). Thomas was a wealthy merchant of Stamford in the south of Lincolnshire, and it is not unreasonable to suggest that this may have been where Francis was born.

Virtually nothing is known of Francis' childhood years. However, it is certain that this was a very difficult and uncertain time, with England in the grip of the Protestant Reformation. A number of important reforms were introduced in Edward's reign, which ended prematurely with his death in 1553. He was succeeded by his half-sister, Mary, who was a committed Catholic and intent on reinstating Catholicism in England. In a short reign, marked by savagery and violence, Mary failed in her bid to reverse the Protestant reforms, and she died in 1558 with her ambitions unrealised. She was succeeded by her half-sister, Elizabeth, a queen who would prove to be shrewder, tougher and longer-lived.

In the same year that Mary died, when Francis Trigge would have been aged 11 or so, his father also died. In his will, recently discovered in the Lincolnshire Archives, Thomas Trigge bequeathed a substantial fortune to his son with the proviso that his mother held it in trust until he reached his 18th birthday.

In 1564 Trigge went up to University College, Oxford where he studied theology. In his second undergraduate year he inherited his father's fortune, but this does not seem to have interfered with his studies. The entry in the monumental *Alumni Oxoniensis* indicates that Trigge was awarded a BA degree in 1568, and an MA degree 1572. At this point most of his contemporaries would expect to be ordained and take up positions as priests in the Church of England but Trigge, as a young man of independent means, decided to remain at his college where he would in due course be elected a Fellow. In the account rolls of University College published by the Oxford Historical Society, a more detailed picture of Trigge's life in the college emerges. To quote, Trigge's life revolved around '…the chapel, where Holy Communion was celebrated in the new orthodox Protestant fashion, on major festivals only: Palm Sunday, Easter, Whitsun and

Fig. 5: The inner gatehouse and part of the curtain wall of Buckden Palace built in 1480 by John Russell, Bishop of Lincoln (1480-1494). His coat of arms can be seen over the gatehouse arch. Francis Trigge was ordained in the Palace chapel.

Christmas; the kitchen, with its massive oven and range, and the pewter dishes from which they ate; the library, which was given a new floor and for which books were sent from London; and the quadrangle, with its grass that needed scything and the ancient apple tree which was cut down and chopped up in 1582.[3] Such a quiet and ordered life appeared to have suited Trigge very well.

In the early 1580s all that changed. Trigge's mother had remarried, her second husband being John Hussey, who became lord of the manor of Honington just outside Grantham in 1583. His family had acquired some status in the late medieval and early modern period, in particular through his forebear, Sir William Hussey. Sir William had been M.P. for Grantham in 1467 and attorney-general under Edward IV in 1471, before rising to the position of Chief Justice of the King's Bench in 1481.[4]

---

3   Quotation from the unpublished notes of Dr Nicholas Bennett, former Librarian of Lincoln Cathedral.
4   Holley, B.J. (2002), *English History Reflected in a Lincolnshire Village*. Honington: Privately Published.

John Hussey's cousin, Charles Hussey, was the patron of the Parish of Welbourn, and was responsible for the selection of a new incumbent for the parish when a vacancy occurred in 1582. He offered Trigge the position and, in due course, Trigge decided to give up his academic life at Oxford for the life of a parish priest in Lincolnshire.

First though was the matter of Trigge's ordination into the priesthood. The Acts of Bishop Thomas Cooper can be found among the records of the Diocese of Lincoln preserved in the Lincolnshire Archives, from which it is apparent that on the morning of 6th February 1583 Trigge was ordained deacon in the chapel of the bishop's palace at Buckden, near Huntingdon (Fig. 5). The records then go on to relate that Trigge was priested in the afternoon of the same day. The register also records that less than two months later, on 24th April 1583, Trigge was installed as Rector in St Chad's Church, Welbourn (Fig. 6).

Nothing in the records provides a clear picture of Trigge's ministry in Welbourn, but it is possible to infer that he was a remarkable parish priest. The Church of England, established by the Elizabethan Settlement of 1559, was Protestant and reformed on the one hand but still retained some key elements of the medieval Church on the other. But there were some who wished to take the process of reform much further. They became known as Puritans and Trigge was numbered among its adherents, as were the Hussey family with which he was now associated.

However, the focus of Trigge's desire for reform was not solely directed at the Church. He was opposed to the practice of enclosure, by which landowners would assume ownership of common land and convert it from arable to rough pasture for sheep farming. Where landowners undertook these enclosures unilaterally, a number of villages were simply abandoned.

In 1594 Trigge published the text of a discourse he had given in St. Wulfram's Church in 1592 entitled *A Godly and Fruitfull Sermon preached at Grantham* by Francis Trigge. In this he described the condition of agriculture and commerce in Lincolnshire. In 1604, he wrote *To the King's Most Excellent Majestie. The Humble Petition of Two Sisters, the Church and Commonwealth. For the restoring of their ancient Commons and Liberties.* This was a vehement protest against enclosure of common land and its consequences, noting the adverse effects it had on the rural population.

Trigge also continued in his role as an educator, especially in ensuring that the curates who worked under him were suitably instructed. The Diocesan archives mention the names of a succession of curates: Ralph Leaver (1596-1603), Nicholas Martin (1591-1595), John Rollinson

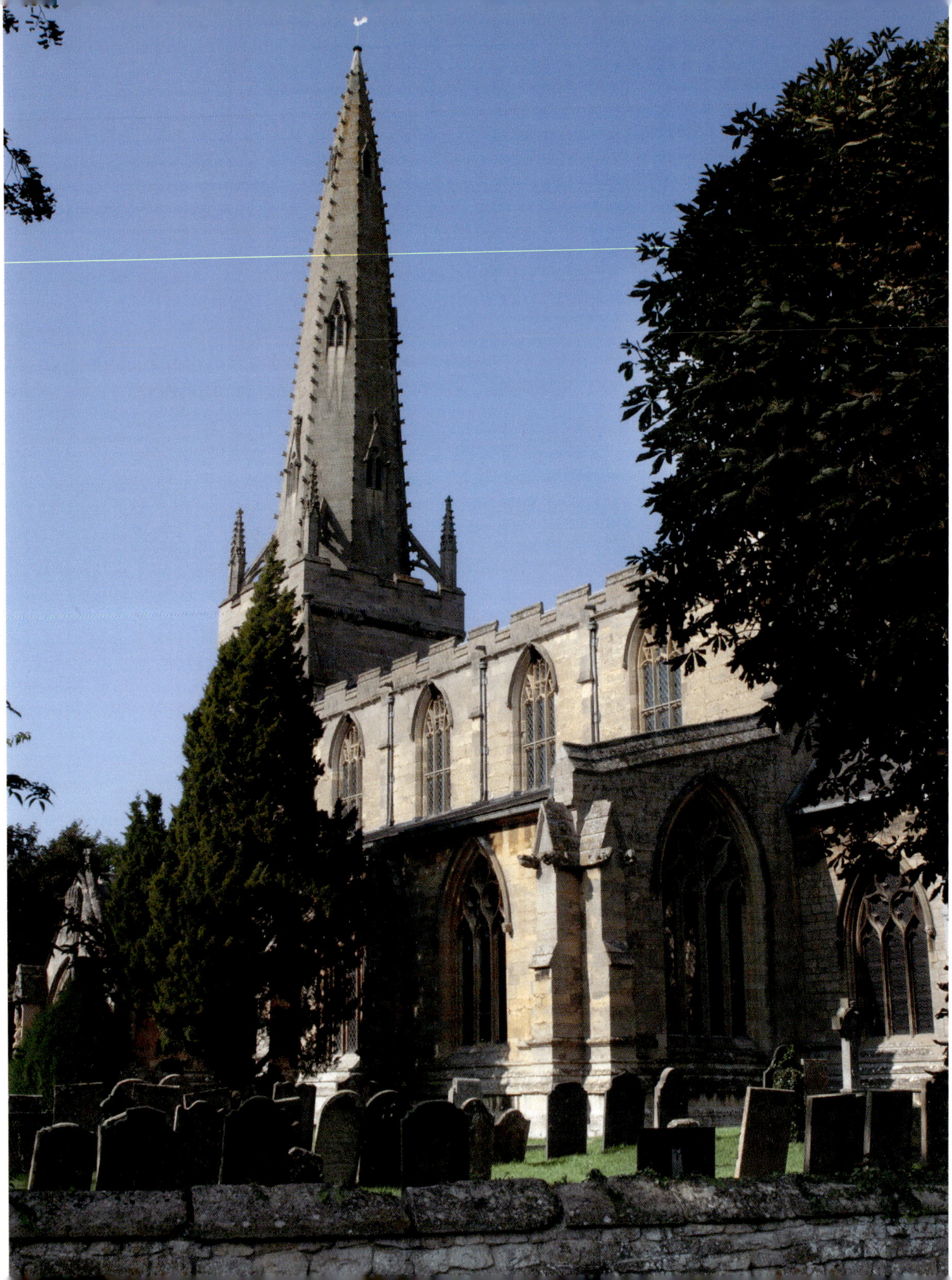

Fig. 7: St. Wilfrid's Church, Honington where Francis Trigge's step-father and mother are buried.

(1596-1603), Simon Read (1604-1606) and Henry Smith (1607). In his will, Trigge bequeathed books from his collection to Simon Read and Henry Smith.

So, as well as his role as a parish priest and rural economist, Trigge acquired a reputation as an able teacher. He gave his curates valuable experience of country ministry by becoming what today would be described as a 'training incumbent', centuries before the term was first coined.

Trigge died in 1606 at the age of 59 and, as a mark of the esteem in which his parishioners held him, he was buried beneath the chancel of St. Chad's Church. The same honour had been accorded to his step-father John Hussey (died 1587) and his mother Elizabeth Hussey (died 1597), who were buried beneath the chancel of St. Wilfrid's Church, Honington (Fig. 7).

(Opposite) Fig. 6: St. Chad's Church, Welbourn, where Francis Trigge was Rector (1582-1606).

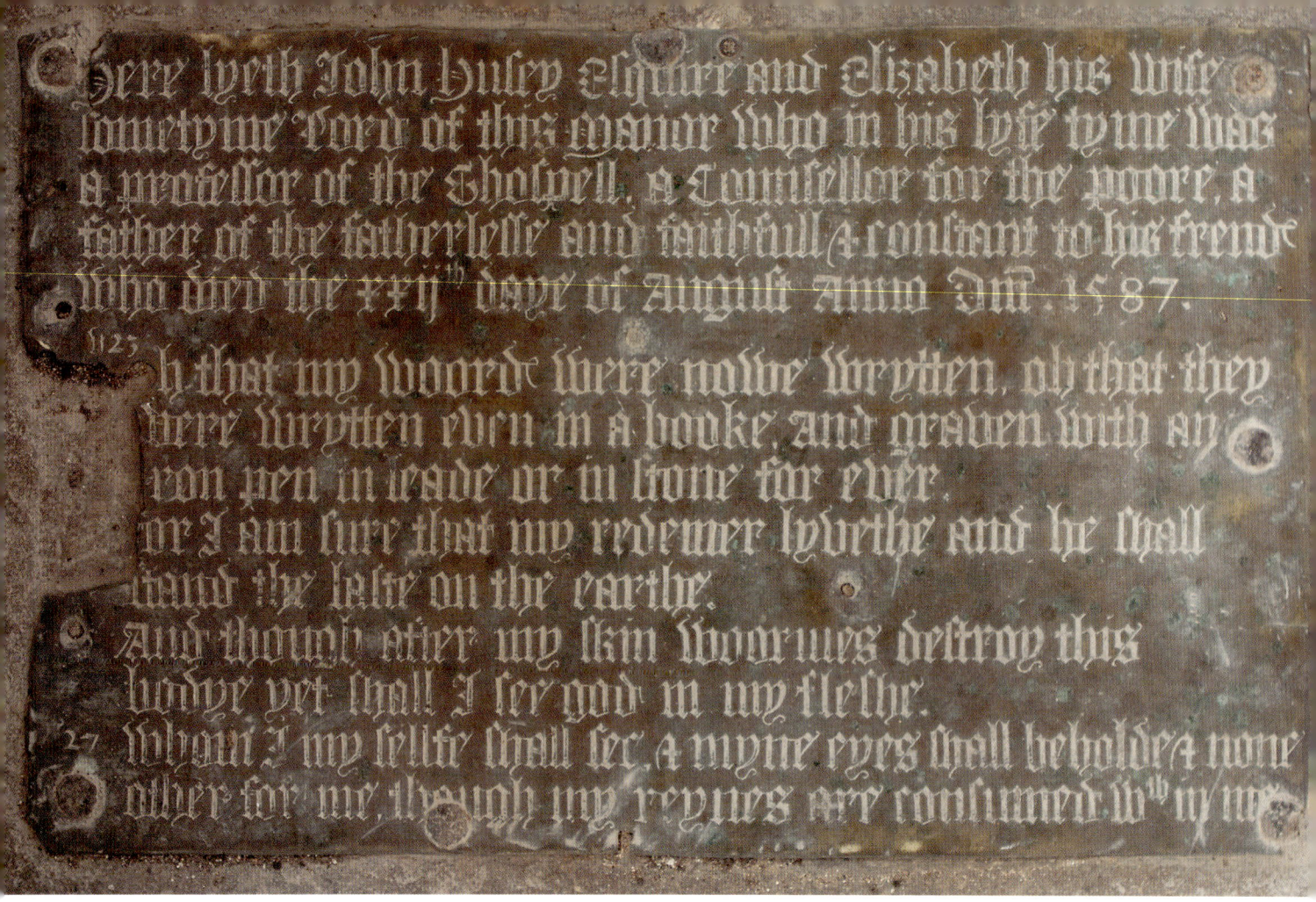

Fig. 8: Brass plaque on the chancel floor of St. Wilfrid's Church, Honington, marking the burial place of Francis Trigges's step-father John Hussey and his mother Elizabeth Hussey.

A brass plaque set into a large stone records this fact (Fig. 8). Unfortunately, in Trigge's case, there is no plaque or stone, but the Library he founded in Grantham surely serves as a reminder of his life and work.

THE BOOKS

So, what is in the Library that is of particular interest? First, there are several incunabula (books printed before 1501) on the shelves. As already noted above, the oldest of these is Lanfranc de Oriano's *Repetitiones*. But the Library's copy of this book also has two other works containing similar legal 'repetitions', bound with it. This was not an uncommon practice, and intended to increase the usefulness of the volume to a potential purchaser. Both of these additions were printed in Naples by Jodocus Hohenstein in about 1476. The first was written by Marianus Soncinus the Elder and entitled *Repetitio capituli "Sententiam sanguinis" super materia irregularitatis*. There are three other recorded copies of this: one (imperfect) in the Biblioteca Capitolare in Atri, Italy; and two in Spain, in Terazona and Valladolid. The other, *Repetitio capituli "Quoniam" de electio* written by Stephanus Caieta, is one of only two copies known to exist, the other being in the John Rylands University Library, Manchester.

Another incunable is the *Imago Mundi* (Fig. 9), originally written in manuscript by Petrus de Alliaco (Pierre d'Ailly) in 1410. The author was Bishop of Cambrai and a Cardinal, but had many other interests including astronomy, mathematics, and navigation. In this book he set out to present the world as he knew it in the early 15th century. It contains several maps and tables of latitude and longitude, and would have been of particular interest to navigators. Therein lies its interest,

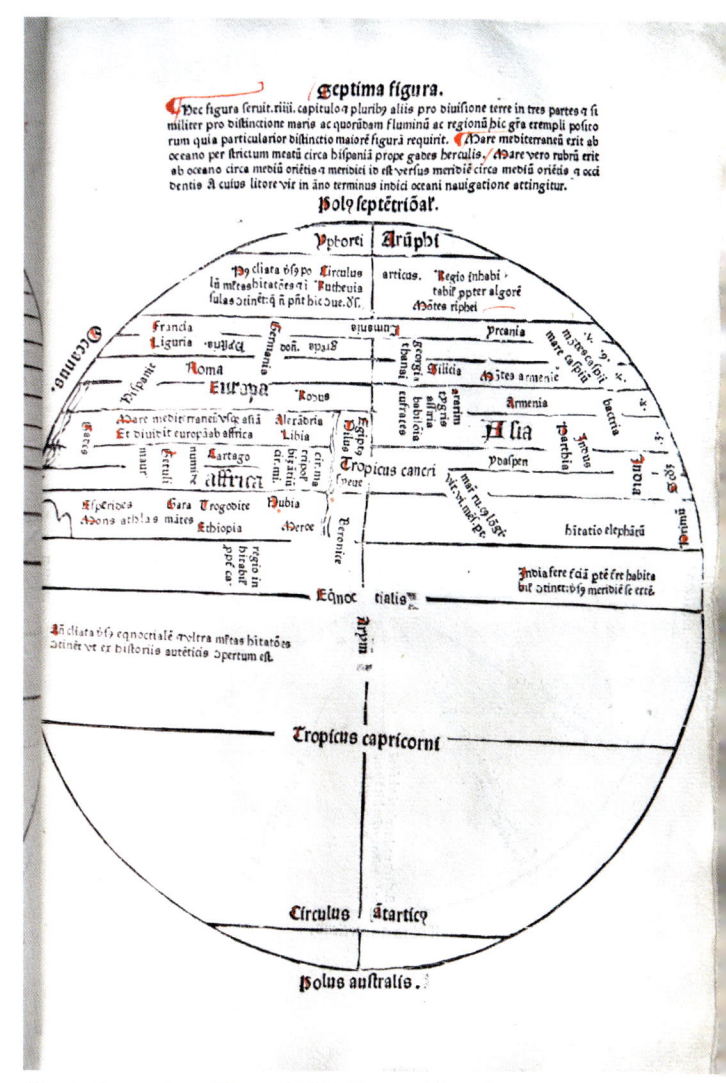

Fig. 9: A page from Pierre d'Ailly's Imago Mundi, *with a map of the Old World. This work was used by Columbus in planning his expedition to discover a new route to the orient.*

because the well-known navigator, Christopher Columbus, purchased a copy. He seems to have read it very thoroughly and annotated its pages with more than 400 marginalia in his own hand. He noted a sentence that translates as: 'The end of the habitable land towards the west and the end of the habitable land towards the east are fairly close, and between them there is little sea'. Columbus became convinced that if he sailed due west from Europe, he could establish a new trade route to the orient, and in 1492 he set off on his epic voyage that would change the course of history.

Columbus' copy of d'Ailly's book can be seen in the Biblioteca Columbina, the remains of a library assembled by his illegitimate son, Hernando Colón, in the thirty years prior to Colón's death in 1539[5]. It is now part of the library of Seville Cathedral.

Pierre D'Ailly's contribution to the early science of astronomy has been recognised by naming one of the craters of the moon, Aliacensis, after him.

One of several books on medicine in the Library is *The Practice of Physick* by Lazare Rivière, printed in London in 1678 by George Sawbridge. Rivière, a professor at the University of Montpellier, was Louis XIII's personal physician. His treatises on remedies for a variety of ailments were very popular and translated into a number of European languages; the Library's English version was the work of the distinguished herbalist and physician, Nicholas Culpeper, and was first published in 1655. Reading this book today suggests that many of the remedies described by Rivière were worse than the conditions they were intended to treat! However, one of the concoctions to combat vomiting described in the book is still used today as Potion of Rivière.

Other medical works include *De re medica* by Aulus Cornelius Celsus, bound with the *De plenitudine* of Galen, both printed in Paris by Christian Welchelus in 1528. These are collections of Roman remedies for various ailments, and their printing date suggests that some were still in use in the 16th century.

A further item with medical connections is four leaves from *De aegritudinibus infantium* by Cornelius Roelans. These were printed in Louvain in 1486, and were subsequently used as the end papers for another book, the *De orthodoxa fide* by John of Damascus, printed in Paris in 1512. Roelans' work, which has not survived, discussed diseases of childhood and other matters related to the care of children. Presumably the bookbinder simply had these to hand and opted to use them in this way!

---

5 Wilson-Lee, E. (2018), *The Catalogue of Shipwrecked Books*. London: Scribner.

Fig. 10: A woodcut of a camel from Conrad Gesner's Historia animalium, *printed in Zurich, 1551-1588*

One of the most interesting and important works in the Library is an incomplete copy of Conrad Gesner's *Historia animalium*, printed in Zurich by Christophe Froschauer in 1551-1588 and bound in two volumes. Gesner was a true polymath whose interests included natural history, bibliography, philology, theology and medicine. He was a life-long practising doctor, and was appointed the City Physician of Zurich in 1554. Nevertheless, he found the time to produce some outstanding publications, including his unique *Bibliotheca universalis* (1545), a catalogue of every writer who had ever lived and their works. But his monumental *Historia animalium* is perhaps the most widely known.

Between 1551 and 1558, Gesner published the first four parts of this encyclopaedia covering all known quadrupeds, amphibia, birds and fish; the fifth part, on snakes and scorpions, was issued posthumously in 1587. In total, the whole work comprised some 4500 pages. Gesner included a number of mythical animals such as the unicorn and the basilisk, but is also credited with providing the first descriptions of the black rat, the guinea pig and the turkey. The whole work was richly illustrated with woodcuts (Figs. 10 & 11), many made by the artist Lucas Schann of Strasbourg, although more recent research indicates that Gesner drew on a large number of other sources for the illustrations.[6]

---

6 Kurasawa, S. (2010), *The Sources of Gesner's Pictures for the Historia Animalium*. Annals of Science, 67(3), 303-328.

De Vlula. Lib.III.

775

DE VPVPA.

Fig 11: A woodcut of an owl from Conrad Gesner's Historia animalium, *printed in Zurich, 1551-1588*

The time in which the *Historia animalium* appeared was marked by a high level of religious tension and this resulted in the work being placed on the Catholic Church's list of banned books. Both Gesner and his printer, Froschauer, were Protestants, and were therefore regarded as being 'contaminated' by heresy. However, this did not prevent the book from being printed and distributed all over Europe.

In 1565, Gesner was in the process of producing a similar encyclopaedia of all known plants, the *Historia plantarum*, when he died from plague at the age of 49. This work, not published until 1754, included the first description of the tulip and in 1753 the Swedish biologist, Carl Linnaeus, named the type species of the *Tulipa* genus *Tulipa gesneriana* in Gesner's honour.

Henry More was born in Grantham in 1614, and attended the Grammar School. He entered Christ's College, Cambridge in 1631, obtained both BA and MA degrees, and immediately afterwards became a Fellow of his college. He established himself as a Neoplatonist philosopher and theologian with interests in natural sciences and taught a number of notable students, including Anne Finch, who later became Lady Conway. It was at her country house in Ragley, Warwickshire that More wrote a number of his books. He also associated with Isaac Newton in Cambridge, although philosophically they had little in common.

In the late 17th century, sometime before his death in 1687, he donated a number of his books to the Library, including one of his most famous works, the *Enchiridion metaphysicum*. In this work More attacked Cartesian philosophy, which in earlier life he had much admired. The Library's copy was printed in 1671 by William Morden in Cambridge.

Although the books in the collection cover a range of subjects, the majority deal with matters of a religious – or, more specifically – Christian nature. One such book is the *Questiones super quattuor libris sententiarum*, written in Oxford by Duns Scotus in about 1300. The edition in the Library was printed in Venice by Bonetus Locatellus in 1497, and is another of the collection's incunabula.

Little is known of Scotus' life, other than that he was a Scottish Catholic priest, a Franciscan friar and a university professor. He worked in Oxford and Paris before moving to Cologne, where he died in 1308. Duns Scotus was given the scholastic accolade Doctor Subtilis (the Subtle Doctor) for his subtle manner of thought.

In this book Scotus argued the limitations of reason in matters of theology, which greatly influenced both religious and secular thinking in Western Europe in the High Middle Ages. He developed doctrines that related to the abstract concepts of existence and individuality as well as metaphysical arguments for the existence of God and the immaculate conception of Mary. He is regarded as one the most important philosopher-theologians of his time, along with Thomas Aquinas and William of Ockham.

The Library's copy of Duns Scotus' remarkable book was one of those bequeathed in the will of Francis Trigge, and so was part of his collection at Welbourn. It would have been placed in the Library sometime after Trigge's death in 1606.

A second book bequeathed by Trigge to the Library was the *Annales ecclesiastici*, written by Caesar Baronius and published in 12 folio volumes between 1588 and 1607. The Library's copy was printed in Mainz by Balthazar Lippius, but consists of only 10 of the 12 volumes.

Baronius was a Catholic priest and ecclesiastical historian who, in 1596, was appointed Cardinal and Librarian of the Vatican. He failed twice in bids to become Pope, largely as the result of his work *On the Monarchy of Sicily* in which he supported papal claims against those of Spain.

The *Annales ecclesiastici* was written in response to the anti-Catholic history *The Magdeburg Centuries* (of which the Library also has a copy), compiled by several Lutheran scholars between 1559 to 1574. The Catholic historian John Dalberg-Acton (1st Baron Acton) described Baronius' book as 'the greatest history of the Church ever written'.

It is often thought that with the advent of printing in the mid-15th century, the production of hand-written manuscripts rapidly declined. But the distinction between print and manuscript was not as clear as it is assumed to have been today. Many printed books had hand-decorated initials to mark the beginning of chapters; and also rubrication where particular passages were marked in red ink. One such book in the Library is a collection of sermons by Leonardo Mattei entitled *Sermones quadragesimales de legibus*, printed in Paris by Ulrich Gehring, Martin Crantz and Michael Friburger in 1477. This has both initials finely decorated in red and blue and rubricated passages.

📖

The writings of several Church Fathers are represented in the Library, but two are of particular interest.

St. John Chrysostom (c.347-407) was for some time Archbishop of Constantinople. He was known for his preaching and public speaking, and the nickname *Chrysostomos* (anglicized as Chrysostom), which means 'golden-mouthed' in Greek, denotes his celebrated eloquence. Chrysostom was among the most prolific authors in the early Christian Church, exceeded only by Augustine of Hippo in the quantity of his surviving writings.

The Library has a copy of his *Opera*, bound as three volumes containing five books and an index. It was printed in Paris by Dionysius Duvallius in 1588 and is noteworthy for the printer's Great Ship device with the arms of Paris and the legend LVTETIA, the Latin name for Paris (Fig 12).

There is also a copy of St. Bernard's *Opera omnia*, consisting of two books bound together in a single volume and printed in Paris by Jacques du Puis, Sebastian Nivelle and Michel Sonnius in 1586, which has the same Great Ship device.

📖

Jean Calvin was a French refugee who fled from France to Geneva in 1535 to escape the violent response of Catholics to the reformers of the Church. He had formerly broken his link to the Catholic Church, possibly in 1533, and converted to the evangelical faith. He became one of the

Fig. 12: The 'Great Ship' printers' mark used by several print shops based in Paris in the late 16th century.

leaders of the Reformation in Western Europe, eventually becoming Moderator of the Genevan Company of Pastors and Chair of Theology at the Genevan Academy.

Calvin produced a large body of written material, particularly collections of sermons and Biblical commentaries. The Library has 14 volumes of his works, mostly in Latin, and many printed in Geneva by Eustathius Vignon. In England, most of these works were available in English by the time the Library was founded, and there are two translations by Arthur Gedding in the collection: *Sermons vpon the booke of Job* and *The Sermons of M. John Caluin upon Deuteronomie gathered by D. Raguenier*. Both were printed in London, the former by T. Dawson in 1579 and the latter by H. Middleton in 1583.

Calvin, who died in 1564, did not live to see the effect of his influence on the Protestant Church and its growth into an international movement. After his death his ideas spread beyond Geneva, and led to the creation of a Christian denomination with its own distinct character.

Calvin was succeeded in both of the posts he held in Geneva by the theologian Theodore Beza. The Library has two of his works: a second edition of *Tractatus theologicarum* printed in Geneva by Eustathius Vignon in 1582; and *In historiam Passionis et sepulturae Domini Nostri Iesu Christi*, also printed in Geneva by Johannes le Preux in 1592.

Not surprisingly, the Library contains a selection of Bibles in various languages, but it might be reasonably argued that the *Polyglot Bible*, printed in Antwerp by Christophe Plantin over the period 1568-1572, is the star attraction of the whole collection. It is certainly widely regarded as one of the finest examples of printing from the 16th century (Fig. 13).

Little is known of Plantin's life. Dirk Imhof[7] has written that 'This is partly down to the paucity of surviving documentation and partly because Plantin was so absorbed in his work that Plantin the man and Plantin the businessman were pretty much one and the same'. By the time (1567) that he conceived the idea of printing a sumptuous polyglot Bible in five languages (Hebrew, Greek, Latin, Aramaic, and Syriac), he already had a well-established and prosperous business in Antwerp employing eight presses (Fig. 14, Fig. 15). However, he knew that in order to realise his ambition he would need to enlarge his printing capacity and have sufficient funds to meet the cost of the new equipment and materials.

---

7 Dirk Imhof is (at the time of writing) the curator of books and archives at the Platin-Moretus Museum in Antwerp.

Fig 13: A page spread from the Polyglot Bible printed by Christopher Plantin in Antwerp, 1568-1573.

Antwerp was, at that time, located in the Spanish Netherlands under the rule of Philip II of Spain, so it was to Philip that Plantin turned for financial support. The king promised to finance the project (hence the Bible is also known as the *Biblia Regia*) and sent the Spanish theologian and scholar Benito Arias Montano to Antwerp to watch over the production of the Bible. By 1574 Plantin had 16 presses in operation and eventually produced 1200 sets on paper and 13 sets on vellum, each set consisting of eight folio volumes. The first four volumes contained the Old Testament; volume V contained the New Testament; volume VI had the complete Bible in the original Hebrew and Greek, as well as an interlinear version that had the Latin translation printed between the lines; and the last two volumes contained dictionaries (Hebrew-Latin, Greek-Latin, Syriac-Aramaic, etc.), grammar rules, lists of names and so on, that would have been of value to scholars.

Unfortunately, the Library has only three volumes of this magnificent work – II, III and IV – but the *Catalogus Librorum* of 1608 (see over) lists all eight volumes as extant. So, what happened to the remaining five volumes?

29

Fig. 14: Interior view of Christopher Plantin's print shop in the Plantin-Moretus Museum, Antwerp (Nina Alizada/Shutterstock).

A record on one of the Benefaction Boards in the ringing chamber of St. Wulfram's Church notes that the three volumes currently in the Library were 'donated' by Robert Sanderson in 1661, shortly after he was appointed Bishop of Lincoln. It is known that, before Sanderson was appointed, he had been working with Peter Walton on the compilation of the equally famous London Polyglot Bible, and possibly borrowed the volumes of the Antwerp Polyglot from the Library to assist with this project. Sanderson then returned three of the volumes and this was subsequently and incorrectly recorded as a gift. If this was the case, then presumably he retained the missing five volumes, the location of which is now unknown. This is, of course, partly speculative and there may be other explanations; but it remains that the connection between these two great Polyglots is intriguing.

A complete copy of the Bible is on display at the Plantin-Moretus Museum in Antwerp (Fig. 16), including the typefaces which were specially designed for the project.

Fig. 15: Original 16th century printing press displayed in the Plantin-Moretus Museum, Antwerp. Most of the books in the Trigge Library were printed on this type of press (Joost Adriaanse/Shuttterstock).

After Trigge's death in 1606 a *Catalogus Librorum* was produced, which listed the contents of the Library at that date. It was hand-written in a legible cursive script on parchment, signed (the signature cannot now be deciphered) and dated February 1608. It is now in the Lincolnshire Archives. A modern catalogue was produced by John Glenn and David Walsh in 1988[8]. Comparison of this with the *Catalogus* shows that only twenty books have been 'lost' from the shelves – a respectable retention of stock for a library now more than 400 years old!

---

8   Glenn, J. & Walsh, D. (1988), *Catalogue of the Francis Trigge Chained Library, St Wulfram's Church, Grantham*. Cambridge: D.S. Brewer

Fig. 16: Exterior view of Christopher Plantin's print shop and publishing house, now the Plantin-Moretus Museum, Antwerp (Pecold/Shutterstock).

EPILOGUE

The Liberal politician Herbert Samuel (1st Viscount Samuel) once described a library as 'thought in cold storage'[9]. This is certainly true of those libraries created to preserve for posterity the works of those whose knowledge and ideas influenced the history and culture of earlier generations. Francis Trigge's Library is one such example.

The opening of the Library at the end of the 16th century followed a period of 150 years that had seen many major changes. After an uncertain start in the 15th century, the art of printing had spread throughout Europe and printing businesses were established in almost every town and city. The days of the scribe carefully copying text by hand were soon numbered as book production moved to the printer's workshop. Most importantly, however, books could be mass-produced and widely distributed, bringing new ideas and concepts to a broader audience.

But libraries, by their very nature, were also vulnerable to natural disaster and human aggression. The period immediately preceding Trigge's birth, the beginnings of the English Reformation, had been marked by the systematic destruction of the great monastic libraries. It is estimated that as a result of this act of mass vandalism tens of thousands of manuscripts and books were burnt or broken up for scrap. The contemporary churchman, historian and writer John Bale wrote: 'To destroy all without consideration, is and will be unto England for ever, a most horrible infamy... What may bring our realm to more shame and rebuke, than to have it known abroad, that we are despisers of learning.'[10]

In spite of this, the advent of the hand-press book certainly benefitted the creation of new libraries and the addition of new books to those that were already established. Those with the necessary financial means acquired private collections, and from the 16th through to the 19th century substantial libraries were a feature of the great (and even relatively modest) country houses that appeared during this period. The properties currently owned by the National Trust – more than 140 of them – house libraries with in excess of 400,000 titles. The once widely-held view that the

---

[9] Samuel, H. (1947), *A Book of Quotations*, p.10, quoted in Partington, A. (Ed.) (1992), *The Oxford Dictionary of Quotations* (Fourth Edition). Oxford: Oxford University Press.

[10] For a full account see Ovendon, Richard (2020) *Burning the Books: A History of Knowledge Under Attack*. London: John Murray.

books in such collections were purchased for show is largely unjustified and, in many cases, it is apparent that the owners displayed considerable taste and discernment in their selection.

Institutional libraries were also formed or expanded. In the year that Trigge published his indenture, Sir Thomas Bodley offered to fund the re-establishment of the library in the University of Oxford. This became the famed Bodleian Library which by 1620, when the librarian Thomas James published the second edition of the library's catalogue, had more than 16,000 books on its shelves.

At the time of its foundation, though, Francis Trigge's Library was unique – it was the first public reference library in the country. How widely it was used cannot now be established but, judging from the number of donations made in the 17th century, it was still well-respected. It survived possible ruin during the Civil War and then suffered a long period of neglect and decay through the 18th and 19th centuries. Fortunately, there were those who eventually recognised its historical and cultural worth, and it was rescued and restored to what the visitor can see today. Stewardship of the Library using professional conservation skills and new technology will ensure that it continues to be maintained and preserved to the highest standards into the future.

To visitors, from wherever you have come and whatever your interest – whether as a scholar, bibliophile or passer-by – you are very welcome. We hope you find your visit interesting and that you will learn something of value, for it is for you that Francis Trigge created the Library in the latter days of the first Elizabethan age.

ACKNOWLEDGEMENTS

I owe debt of gratitude to a number of people without whom this Guide might not have seen the light of day. In particular, I would like to thank my ever-patient wife, Sue, for reading every draft and for her proof-reading skill in spotting errors, omissions, and instances of dubious grammar. Any errors that have survived are entirely my own.

I am also grateful to my friends and colleagues Dr. John Manterfield, Dr. Anke Timmermann and Mark James for their interest and valuable input at a difficult time in all our lives. In addition, various parts of the Guide have been brought to life by Roger Sleigh's splendid photographs, and I am greatly indebted to him.

I acknowledge the generosity of Dr. Nicholas Bennett who provided access to his invaluable notes on the life and times of Francis Trigge, and for allowing me to quote from them.

My thanks are due to Mike Sinclair of The Artworker and Ron Naylor of Flexpress Ltd., whose creativity and skill turned my ideas into reality.

The Rector of St Wulfram's Church, Fr. Stuart Cradduck, and the Churchwardens have been, and continue to be, very supportive of all those who are privileged to care for the Trigge Library. I am also indebted to the Friends of St Wulfram's Church who kindly provided financial support for the production of this Guide.

Finally, I have been inspired by the writings of the late John Glenn, who first created a guide book of the Library that has been in circulation for many years. Together with David Walsh, John also published the definitive modern catalogue of the books in the Library. I hope this Guide has done him justice.

Brian Stagg (*Custos*)
The Trigge Library
St. Wulfram's Church, Grantham
January 2021

Front Cover: The Trigge Library in the room over the south porch of St. Wulfram's Church, including one of the bookcases and a 17th century table and chair.

Back Cover: Christopher Plantin's printers' mark.